AF265254

AFTERCARE: 21 THINGS TO DO AFTER SEX

Because endings matter

STACEY HERRERA

Copyright © 2020 by Stacey Herrera

All rights reserved. No part of this publication may be reproduced, distributed or transmitted in any form or by any means, including photocopying, recording, or other electronic or mechanical methods, without the prior written permission of the publisher, except in the case of brief quotations embodied in critical reviews and certain other noncommercial uses permitted by copyright law. For permission requests, write to the author, at:

Stacey Herrera / The Sensuality Project

stacey@staceyherrera.com

Ordering Information:

Quantity sales. Special discounts are available on quantity purchases by corporations, associations, and others. For details, contact: admin@thesensualityproject.com

Aftercare: 21 Things to Do After Sex/ Stacey Herrera. —1st ed.

Print ISBN: 978-0-578-74656-2 / Ebook ISBN: 978-1-0878-9777-6

To Chris + West,

Thank you for holding space for my intentions and giving me space to birth this book.

I am forever changed. ♥

Introduction

The most important part of sex is underrated — aftercare. Because no matter how great the sex is, if it ends poorly, that's what you'll remember.

This applies to almost everything. If someone lives a great life and dies a horrific death, people will focus on their death. If you're in a loving relationship and the other person grows distant and cold, you'll remember the shivers. Have you ever seen a great movie that is ruined in the final scene? That's the worst, right?! The bottom line is endings matter.

I am of the mind that aftercare is something that should be practiced regularly —by everyone. Whether you are having kinky sex, vanilla sex, penetration-less sex, or dry-humping, aftercare should never be optional.

As a best practice, I encourage you to ask your partner in advance, *"how do you like to be cared for after sex?"* This will ensure that they enjoy themselves from start to finish — which is good for them and for you.

It's worth noting that some people do not require any form of aftercare whatsoever. So if your partner would rather not be touched or prefers to be left entirely alone after sex - honor that. Sometimes the ideal post-coital activity is doing absolutely nothing. And if that's the case, it's still aftercare, and it counts.

But if you and your partner enjoy *the sexy time after sexy time*, this tiny book for you.

ONE

Pee

This might seem obvious, but peeing after sex is essential. Because the odds of developing a UTI (urinary tract infection) is are greater after you've been getting busy. This is true for vulva and penis owners. So while peeing is not a "together" activity per se, believe me when I say it's mutually beneficial.

Cover the Wet Spot

Sex gets messy, and bodies produce fluids. Sometimes those fluids coalesce in one spot — the wet spot. And trust me, nobody wants to lie in the wet spot. So cover it up. A towel or a t-shirt will do. Your partner will thank you.

Talk

Post-copulation convos enhance intimacy. It doesn't have to be heavy or complicated. But light conversation after sex is often reassuring, and it can also reduce post-sex anxiety, which is totally a thing.

Eat

Sex is exercise, and exercise can make you hungry. And a post-sex snack is a great way to unwind - together.

Shower

A post-nookie shower is a fantastic way to keep the physical and emotional intimacy going. Plus, water is soothing to the nervous system. That sounds like a win-win to me.

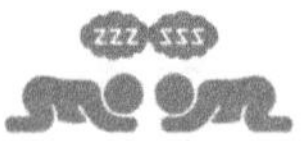

SIX

Nap

During arousal, your body releases dopamine, which is a neurotransmitter that enhances pleasure. But post-coital, your body releases oxytocin, a hormone that aids in relaxation, which is why you might feel compelled to drift off to la-la-land. Catching some zzz's with or without a partner is a great way to take care of yourself.

Massage

Offering a massage to your partner is a beautiful way to express love, care, and appreciation. Massages soothe the body and the mind, all while deepening intimacy and connection.

Listen to Music

Sex may be a physical act, but it also has an emotional impact. So if you ever find yourself speechless after a beautifully intense sexual experience, let the music speak for you. Even songs without lyrics have a lot to say.

Aftercare Playlist

Dance Naked

A naked dance party is a great way to keep the sexual energy moving! You can dance fast or slow. Together or separate. In the dark or with the lights on. Lovers choice!

Eat Ice Cream

Eating ice cream after sex is just the right thing to do. You can feed one another or enjoy separately-together while playing footsie under the covers. Good times, delicious vibes, excellent company, BIG WIN!

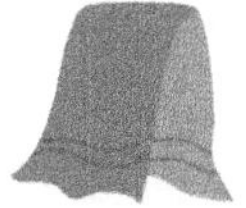

Warm Towel

A warm towel after sex is the gift you always needed but didn't know you wanted. A warm towel says, "you matter," and "I care." And it makes your genitals happy too.

Write Invisible Notes

Write an invisible note on your partner's body. The sensation of tracing lines with your fingers will be soothing and sweet. This is the stuff that memories are made of.

Read Poetry

Few things are more soothing than having someone read to you, except maybe having someone read poetry to you after sex. Yeah, that. It's all the things - literally.

Have a Picnic

Having a picnic in the middle of the bed. It's sort of like building a bed-fort, but way better —because FOOD!

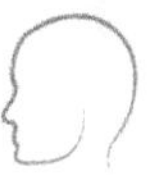

Scalp Massage

Scalp massages are very relaxing. Because when the scalp is stimulated, it also relieves tension in the neck and shoulders. All while calming the nervous system. Definitely, a must-do.

Kiss em' All Over

After spending time making love with your boo, you feel all romantic, you know? The electricity that I like call passion permeates the air, which puts you in a mood (and sometimes "the mood). And so what do you do with all that feel-goodness? Kiss em' all over! Keep stoking that love fire for as long as you can.

Tea Time

There is something about sitting down for a cuppa post-sex that is so soothing. Especially when it's cold out —as if you needed another reason to snuggle up close to your boo, right?

Gratitude

Gratitude is, by far, the best and most crucial aftercare practice. Expressing gratitude helps to fortify positive emotions and experiences. It also boosts confidence and improves overall wellbeing. Sorta like emotional Vitamin C!

Cook Together

Sex is one that people get some, not all, of their emotional needs, met. It's all about connection, right? Well, cooking together is like that too! And if you do it after sex, you're like DOUBLE winning! Cooking creates positive memories, strengthens bonds, and nourishes each person emotionally. That's what's up!

Touch Their Genitalia

Genitals can be very sensitive post-orgasm. But if your partner is up for it, a light, gentle touch can feel really good. It's an act of reassurance and can serve as a building block to intimacy long after sex is done.

Cuddle-up

Post-coital affection will help you and your partner to feel more grounded. Because when sex is over, the entire body goes through the refractory period. The comedown, after so much stimulation, can be overwhelming. And that's true for people with penises too. But staying in physical contact can help to ease that transition, physically and emotionally.

If you enjoyed this book, you should totally sign up for my newsletter. I share relationship-ing stories, intimacy tips, articles, and other useful things.

And while you're at it, download this free relationship check-up worksheet, which is another excellent aftercare activity.

You're welcome!

Appreciation

Jamee, Niara, & Alaina, for being a constant source of inspiration, love, and entertainment. There is never a dull moment!

Mark & Francisco for practicing aftercare and all the stuff that comes before that with me.

Alex & Lindsey, for your endless support and encouragement, I couldn't have written this book without you.

And for all you lovers out there, for prioritizing pleasure and happy endings - you're amazing!

About the Author

Stacey Herrera is an intimacy + relationship coach, writer, and creator of The Sensuality Project. Through her sensuality focused work, she helps humans explore their sexuality, enhance intimacy, and create deliciously fulfilling relationships.

Her #1 mission in life is to master the art of "relationshiping," because she believes that connection is magical, and INTIMACY is the holy grail.

She lives in the Port of Los Angeles. You can read her musings on Medium @StaceyHerrera

Sites & Resources

Here is list of the site address listed in this book:

Aftercare Play List:
https://staceyherrera.com/aftercareplaylist

Newsletter:
https://bit.ly/StaceyMails

Relationship Check-up Worksheet:
https://staceyherrera.com/checkup

The End

www.ingramcontent.com/pod-product-compliance
Lightning Source LLC
Chambersburg PA
CBHW051014050726
47592CB00007B/2841